BUDAPEST
Through My Lens

A SOLITARY PERSPECTIVE

Dear Roz!

Greetings from Budapest!

via Ashokan!

Hope to see you here someday!

Stephen Spinder

Ashokan 2000007. 12.31

PUBLISHED BY:	STEPHEN SPINDER FINEART PHOTOGRAPHY
HUNGARY OFFICE:	1062 Budapest, Bajza utca 54. II/1b Phone: +36 (1) 331-2601 Fax: +36 (1) 331-2601 Mobile: +36 (70) 214-7221
NORTH AMERICA OFFICE:	119 Hidden Valley Road Rochester, N.Y. 14624 Phone: 585 247 7956

Website: **www.spinderartphoto.com**
E-mail: **stephen@spinderartphoto.com**

All photographs in this book were made by the artist using KODAK black and white and color analog films. They were created and composed in the camera, without manipulation, or digital alteration.

Fifth edition. October 2005.

First printed in Hungary. October 2002.
© Stephen M. Spinder 2005

EDITING *Heather Hermant*

LAYOUT, DESIGN: *László Buzás, Stephen Spinder*
GRAPHICS: *László Buzás, Hajnalka Németh*

ISBN 963 204 860-1

PRINTED BY *Folprint Printing House*
(1119 Budapest, Thán Károly utca 23-25. Hungary)

Contents

udapest has many names, faces and moods - the 'Queen of the Danube', 'Paris of the East'. It is a Mecca for visitors and a much loved home for its citizens. Throughout her history the city has inspired and given birth to many famous photographers. I applaud them all for their vision, their dedication to their work and for paving the roads before me. Many books have been written about her charm. It is my pleasure to present another - *Budapest Through My Lens, A Solitary Perspective.*

The inspiration for this book project started when I first travelled to Eastern Europe to chase down Hungarian folk dancing in Transylvania. I had always wanted to publish a book of my work. It never became more of a reality than when I arrived in this city and began to develop the network of friends, colleagues and professionals who have supported me from the beginning. I would like to thank so many people who have, directly and indirectly, been the true architects of this long-incubating publication; without their unselfish giving, relentless energy, and eternal patience in dealing with me, the artist, it could never have happened. To them, I am greatly indebted.

It's people like Irwin Kassai, who greeted me at my first AmCham mixer and introduced me to countless individuals who have since become regulars in my network; Aladár Kard, the voice of Budapest business and diplomatic circles who seems to know everyone in the city at all levels and professions; Péter Fáth, for his endless support and praise of my work which has elevated me to the level of 'well-known' in the international business community, and whose knowledge and fascination with photography far outweigh anything I could ever hope to achieve. Thanks to Ambassador Péter Kraft for his ego-boosting invitation to exhibit at the Hungarian Embassy in Lima, Peru; To Mónika Szente and Ormai és Társai, C'M'S' Cameron McKenna for my first sale, their praise of my work, and their encouragement to continue on my path; Marianne Suto at Kodak for endless rolls of Ektachrome film; Csaba Zsarnowszki at Adeko Moulding for his dealer prices; János Huschit at Lettera for the highest quality, state-of-the-art graphics; Ferenc Nika at Studioline whose great equipment 'deals' allowed me to increase my own profits; Glen Parker at the Marriott Hotel for his protocol gift purchases; Gábor and Attila at Bortársaság (Budapest Wine Society) for generous supplies of quality spirits at the drop of a hat; and György Ifjú formerly of the Budapest Office of Tourism for one of my largest sales and the placement of my work all around Europe.

Acknowledgements

In more recent times, I would like to thank George Herbert Walker, the US Ambassador to Hungary for his kind words of support and presentation of this book to George W. Bush, US President; to Elekes Botond at the Hungarian Ministry of Cultural Heritage for his door-opening purchases for the Ministry of Culture and eventual introduction to Edit Kulcsár, curator/owner of the Vármegye Gallery of Transylvanian artists; Iván Bába formerly State Secretary of the Foreign Ministry for his grand support of my exhibitions in America and the eventual purchase of my work; Mr. Géza Jeszenszky, former Hungarian Ambassador to America and Andras Simonyi, current Ambassador for their purchase of my work; and to Tibor Jack at the Ministry of Foreign Affairs for the purchase and placement of my work in Hungarian Embassies around the world.

I would also like to give great thanks to Heather Hermant for proof-reading, her pain-staking editing and the best informal portrait ever taken of me; to Kerrie and Bill McGann, Pablo Gorondi and Yana Itskovich and Mark Waldman for maintaining the largest private collections of my work. And last, but certainly not least, my gratitude to János Fodor and László Buzás at Folprint Printing for their patient cooperation, dedication and countless hours spent to assure quality, elegance and consistency throughout this publication.

And a last special word of thanks to Natalie Lee, mother of Jonathan, a friend, whom I met by chance one evening in a coffee house during her short time in Budapest. During our visit she provided me with the clever assembly of words that eventually became the title of this long awaited publication.

Some of these people have moved away but they will never be forgotten. They will always be a part of my Budapest – a circle of friends and colleagues who have made my 11 years in this city memorable ones, successful ones and a cornerstone in my development as an artist, a professional, and a person.

In this, my 14th year of photographing the city, I hope you will find my views elegant, unique, sometimes ambiguous, but always fascinating.

Stephen Spinder

Budapest 2005

I first met Stephen during the turn of the year 1996 when he walked into my office at the American Chamber of Commerce to show me his photographs of Budapest and Transylvania. It was love at first sight - his images were stunning! I remember telling him, "Mr. Spinder, you should make a book". He was articulate, humorous and, as an image maker, inspiring.

Soon after that in the Spring of 1997, I was one of two speakers he had arranged for the opening of his first major exhibition in Budapest at the Hyatt Hotel. It was an exquisite showing with 85 people in attendance. Not bad for a foreigner who had just recently arrived in Budapest! I was very impressed with his total organization of the event, and I was equally impressed with the network he had developed in such a short time. However, it was his views of Budapest that most impressed me.

It was not only the quality of his work that inspired me but also the fact that he had images of places what we pass by every day without paying attention to the beauty of them. As a photographer myself, I can appreciate Stephen's eye, his unique viewpoints and sensitivity to the finer details of this fabled urban landscape.

I have been photographing this city for decades and never thought some of the views Stephen was able to capture. Gothic spires with elaborate ornamentation, neo-Classic facades, baroque statues emphasizing dramatic, curving forms are all captured in twilight color and elegant black and white, the latter has been sepia-toned to render the feel of the city's 'Golden Age'.

I would be untrue if I didn't mention here that I am most sensitive to Stephen's black and white work. Why? The answer is really rooted in the history of photography. The first color photographic material was only available after 1930 or so. Stephen's images have the feel of being made at the turn of the century. His photos are much more artistic; they don't show reality. Rather, they express feelings, abstractions and opinions of the artist. With color photographs the color depicts a real object; we naturally see the world in color and this can get in the way of witnessing a really great artistic image. Black and white reduces the image to the most basic elements of artistic vision - composition, contrast, textures, patterns and the play of light on a surface. It helps make the distinction between real object and art easier to see.

For me, it is a double pleasure to introduce his book. I appreciate Stephen's vision and his recognition of photography as a field of art. It is a vision we share. Will he ever reach the status of the greatest Hungarian photographers – Brassai, Kertész, Moholy-Nagy? Probably not, but his sensitivity, vision and accomplishments can be appreciated just the same.

Due to his recent exhibitions at the Hungarian Embassy in Washington DC., and the Hungarian Consulate in New York City, as well as being honored at this year's Budapest International Spring Festival, his work has been celebrated internationally. However, this was not the first time. His work has been on display at the American/Hungarian Museum in New Brunswick since 1995. He has shown at the Hungarian House in New York City and was included in a major exhibition in Rochester, New York - his home town. In 1999, he was invited to show at the prestigious October 23rd Ceremonies at Indiana University, and in 2000 at the Hungarian Museum in Cleveland Ohio. Last year he was guest artist at the annual Western Canadian Hungarian Dance/Folk Art Festival in Calgary, and this year, in 2002 in Winnipeg.

Stephen usually sets out to wander through Budapest with his camera at a time when the city is preparing for the night or when the city is not quite awake. His aim is not to photograph as many of Budapest's remarkable sites as possible, but rather to portray - always in a different light - the feeling and the sense of history that dominates the city's abundance of architectural styles. Intricate details, interiors and exteriors are all convincingly documented by the black and white photography of Stephen Spinder.

I encourage you to have a long look at his images, perhaps more than once, and see how much more appears in your eye and in your heart with each viewing.

Executive Director, American Chamber of Commerce

Budapest Through My Lens

A Solitary Perspective

PART ONE | DUOTONE PLATES

Gellért from Behind

1997

A monument like this deserves a lot of exploration. History has it that Gellért, a Venetian bishop, was thrown off the cliff in 1046 while trying to convert the pagan Magyars to Catholicism. Looking through this imposing complex, one can see many of the sites on the Pest side.

Stephen Spinder
Budapest
Through My Lens

A Solitary Perspective

*T*urul

1999

Standing guard on Castle Hill, is this mighty mythical bird said to have grandfathered Árpád, founder of the first Hungarian dynasty. Ironically, this dramatic people-less photo was made during the annual, and packed, St. Stephen's Day Buda Castle Arts Festival! Just after sunset I struggled through the crowd to the food (and beer!) booth. Looking up, I caught the turul in rapidly changing twilight.

STEPHEN SPINDER

BUDAPEST
THROUGH MY LENS
A Solitary Perspective

Gateway to the Royal Palace

1997

The Royal Palace atop Castle Hill is surrounded by elaborately decorated stone walls and wrought iron gates. I ventured up here one morning in a light fog and was fortunate to find a 'white seamless background' behind everything I framed. These amazing ornate gates and the mighty *Turul* which sits atop the massive ramparts, guard the entrance to the main courtyard and retain the atmosphere and memories of the medieval capital.

STEPHEN SPINDER
BUDAPEST
THROUGH MY LENS
A Solitary Perspective

Danube through Chain Bridge

1996

As I walked across the Chain Bridge, looking south it seemed as if I was looking at Budapest through a big open window. The strong vertical lines and the classic, recognizable shape of the lamps made this one of my most popular earlier photos.

*G*ellért Baths Lobby

1997

The unparalleled beauty, elegant symmetry, and grandeur of this building interior are equalled only by the achievement of capturing it all without people in view... Looking down from the second floor, I was fascinated by the curves and the contrasts of light and dark. If only I could

make all those people go away. Within seconds, a clearing
appeared as the gaggle of tourists vacated the room, my
good fortune.

STEPHEN SPINDER
BUDAPEST
THROUGH MY LENS
A Solitary Perspective

Chain Bridge with Snow

1999

I awoke one morning to find newly fallen white stuff blanketing the city. From experience I knew that fresh snow doesn't last long in Budapest. This typical view from Pest is immensely more interesting when covered with snow; the bridge becomes glorified with a cold stark reality.

STEPHEN SPINDER

BUDAPEST
THROUGH MY LENS
A Solitary Perspective

*T*hrough Spires of
Inner Parish Church

1997

I can't quite remember where I took this shot from, but I remember being struck by the delicate Freedom Statue framed by the massive towers. Perhaps it was from the third floor of ELTE University at March 15 square.

Clock Tower, St. Anne's Church

2000

From a series. Throughout my photographic career, I have always had a fascination with clock towers. This is probably because as an artist I have such a difficult relationship with time. This church is right at Batthyány ter on the Buda side.

STEPHEN SPINDER
BUDAPEST
THROUGH MY LENS
A Solitary Perspective

Parliament Building

1996

Symbol of the capital, this building (268 meters) celebrated its 100 year anniversary in 2002. Without its scaffolding – a permanent part of this facade since the first time I saw it in 1991 – one can see the unbroken line of arcades dominating the building. In black and white, the neo-Renaissance and neo-Gothic motifs stand out more clearly than the color original of this image.

*K*ings,
Heroes' Square

1997

This massive complex of statues and buildings at the head of Andrássy street is one of the most impressive sights of Budapest. For me, it is a compositional dream, with its strong vertical lines and juxtaposed organic curves. The dark sky was enhanced by the standard tool in my black and white arsenal, the red filter.

Inscriptions, Heroes' Square

1997

These words were carved on the Tomb Of The Unknown Soldier. It is in memory of all the people who gave their lives in the defense of freedom, liberty and independence. I speak in the past because although the large tomb is still there, the words have been removed and a short wrought iron gate now surrounds the tomb.

STEPHEN SPINDER
BUDAPEST
THROUGH MY LENS
A Solitary Perspective

Archangel Gabriel, Heroes' Square

1996

In her right hand, the apostolic cross, in her left, the Hungarian crown. I photographed this Millennium Monument often during my first months living in Budapest. From a vantage point somewhere in the skating rink area, I discovered this dynamic perspective, where the 8 meter statues which encircle the 36 meter obelisk, appear taller than the obelisk column itself.

STEPHEN SPINDER
BUDAPEST
THROUGH MY LENS
A Solitary Perspective

Lamp on *Chain Bridge*

1998

Bridges make cities, and this one is King. Three hundred and eighty meters long, this was the first permanent bridge to link Buda and Pest. I wanted to make a new image of this massive structure, highlighting the new Hungarian coat of arms. This shot has become one of my most popular images.

Szabadság Square

1995

Here stands the only remaining memorial to the Soviet soldiers who died during the liberation of Budapest. A glance behind the Iron Curtain reveals the irony in the name, which means 'Freedom Square'.

STEPHEN SPINDER

BUDAPEST
THROUGH MY LENS
A Solitary Perspective

Lion with Parliament

2000

The monolithic, Gothic style Parliament House seems dwarfed here by the equally impressive, yet much smaller, guard lions of the Chain Bridge. Playing with perspective and lens choice, I was able to create this unusual juxtaposition.

STEPHEN SPINDER
BUDAPEST
THROUGH MY LENS
A Solitary Perspective

Great Synagogue Towers

1998

This is the largest synagogue in Europe, and the second largest in the world. For me, it is also the most difficult building in Budapest to photograph from the right angle. There are telephone wires, other buildings, and overhead tramlines disturbing the composition. I entered a building across Károly körút and began knocking on doors, until I found one kind resident who allowed me to hang out his window for 1/25th of a second.

STEPHEN SPINDER

BUDAPEST
THROUGH MY LENS
A Solitary Perspective

Holocaust Memorial Tree

2001

On my obligatory tourist visit, I got inside and up close to this incredibly detailed monument. Thousands and thousands of leaves on this memorial are inscribed with the names of those who perished in the Holocaust. It is an enormously impressive reminder, with its shiny surfaces glistening like gold in the summer sun, almost blinding the viewer.

STEPHEN SPINDER

BUDAPEST
THROUGH MY LENS
A Solitary Perspective

Anna Café, Vörösmarty Square

1997

After showing my Budapest portfolio to a client, I was asked if I had any shots of this café. "Why?" I asked. I decided the best view of this tourist site would be from above. A very distinguished gentleman answered the first door I knocked on across the square, and graciously welcomed me to his second floor livingroom window.

STEPHEN SPINDER
BUDAPEST
THROUGH MY LENS
A Solitary Perspective

Vígszínház

2000

The Comedy Theater is one of the most elaborate, ornate buildings in Budapest. I have photographed the front, the sides, the top and the middle; details, statues, full shots and the entrance way. From every angle, this building provides interesting compositions. Of course, I hadn't tried the night shot yet...

O*pera House*

1998

With properly pre-visualized exposure compensation, a silhouette can be created almost anywhere there is a strong bright light. With my polarizer filter, I was able to intensify the tone of the blue sky and provide a flat background for the gleaming bright white statues of Beethoven, Mozart, Rossini, Moussorgsky and Tchaikovsky.

STEPHEN SPINDER
BUDAPEST
THROUGH MY LENS
A Solitary Perspective

Keleti Trabant

1991

Budapest's eastern train station has had a face lift since this shot was made. This old relic of a car, as if abandoned, offers a kind of face from that past era. You can almost hear that characteristic Trabant sound, the sputter and cough of its old engine right before it collapses.

Trabants and Ladas

1991

As I waited on top of the Hotel Intercontinental for a sunset, I noticed the traffic patterns leading under the Chain Bridge. It reminded me of a composition I made in Nepal of a meandering herd of goats being 'funnelled' across a single lane bridge.

These are the cars of my early days in Budapest, the ones
that are rapidly disappearing into nostalgia.

Liberty through Elizabeth Bridge

1996

One of seven bridges to span the Danube, the Elizabeth Bridge, named for the beloved Queen Hungarians affectionately call 'Sisi', seems to be composed of tight ropes and trapezes. Its supports offer crisp clean frames from many angles for the goddess atop Gellért Hill.

St. Stephen at Fishermen's Bastion

1997

Never one of my favorites, this shot was discovered on my contact sheets by a client. It's one of the few photographs I have of Budapest with people in it. They appear a necessary part of the composition, as if King St. Stephen watches over them. The bastion was built a century ago to celebrate the 1000th anniversary of the Magyars' arrival in Europe.

_K_ossuth at Parliament

_1997_

Lajos Kossuth was a lawyer and editor of the radical newspaper _Pesti Hírlap_. He was also a statesman of the 1848 Hungarian revolution against the Habsburg monarchy. Kossuth symbolically addresses the nation from his permanent perch overlooking the Parliament at the square that bears his name.

STEPHEN SPINDER
BUDAPEST
THROUGH MY LENS
A Solitary Perspective

Gellért Monument in Snow

2000

On another rare occasion, snow fell in Budapest and covered the city in white for a few hours. I ran to one of my favorite locations. From below, the Bishop seemed so tranquil. I tried several angles but settled on this one to emphasize the vertical element of falling snow.

Stephen Spinder

Budapest
Through My Lens
A Solitary Perspective

Vörösmarty Square, Lamp Post

1995

When I first moved to Budapest, I was shooting for the English language telephone book. Although this is one from the series that didn't make it into the book, I have always liked the intricate strength of the lamps that decorate the fountains here.

STEPHEN SPINDER
BUDAPEST
THROUGH MY LENS
A Solitary Perspective

Beauties on Buildings

1996

If you look up while strolling the wide boulevards of Pest, you will find these beauties gracing many Budapest facades. Another one of my unrecognizable viewpoints even to native Budapesters, I found these by looking north from the bridge crossing over Nyugati square. Cropped as I was by traffic on the sidewalk-less bridge, I also did a little cropping. There is a large neon Nokia sign just above the heads of these statues.

STEPHEN SPINDER
BUDAPEST
THROUGH MY LENS
A Solitary Perspective

View from the top

1991

Upon completing a self-negotiated route to the rooftop of Atrium Hyatt Hotel, I waited two hours to make a sunset shot. It's views like this one that illustrate architectural richness of the Hungarian capitol. The location of this

composition is my most obscure, and I leave it to the viewer to discover from where it was taken.

STEPHEN SPINDER

BUDAPEST
THROUGH MY LENS
A Solitary Perspective

$\mathcal{F}$reedom Bridge

1999

Two more *turul* (mythical bird) watch over the city from their perch on the very top of the bridge. The Szabadsag bridge's rich green contrasts the bright red in the Hungarian coat of arms which adorn the crossbar near the top. The black and white version puts emphasis on the breadth and girth of this massive structure.

*C*hain Bridge, *Lamps and Lions*

1998

Budapest is, in fact, three cities in one officially joined in 1873. This was the first permanent bridge to span the Danube. The lamps seem to form a protective ring around the guard lion.

Rákóczi
at Parliament

2001

Ferenc, Prince of Transylvania was a wealthy aristocrat who led the war of independence against the Habsburgs in 1703. His importance is emphasized by the framing of his massive body by the towers and flags of Parliament.

Árpád in Winter

1998

This Monarch marched on in all seasons and led thousands of his people to their settlements beyond the Carpathians; yet here he seems strikingly solitary wearing a coat of fresh snow under a crisp winter sky.

STEPHEN SPINDER
BUDAPEST
THROUGH MY LENS
A Solitary Perspective

Gresham Facade Detail

1999

With the impending purchase and planned renovation of this turn-of-the-century building, I decided to photograph it before it changed. In Art Nouveau style it was originally built for and by a British Insurance company of the same name.

*G*eological Institute

1997

Many of the roofs of noble buildings in Budapest are adorned with the red, green and gold tiles of the Zsolnay factory. This composition in black and white however emphasizes the organic shapes and forms decorating the roof, leading to the figures holding up the globe.

*P*arliament from Danube Level

1996

Most of my earlier days in Budapest were spent at the banks of the Danube overlooking the spires of Buda. I'd not yet gotten my feet wet shooting the Parliament from the Buda side. This unusual vantage point, right down on the rocks at water level, was captured with a

24mm lens. Being close and seeing Parliament like this captures the feeling of movement in the water without actually being on a boat.

STEPHEN SPINDER
BUDAPEST
THROUGH MY LENS
A Solitary Perspective

Interior of *Parliament*

1999

This was a 'grab' shot taken while on assignment photographing the 10th Anniversary of the American Chamber of Commerce in Hungary. It shows the richly decorated Parliament Chambers where gnome-sized pyrogranite statues, frescos and tapestries depict Hungarian history and legends.

*C*hapel Ják, *Vajdahunyad Castle*

1999

The portal of this chapel is copied from the 13th Century Abbey Church in Ják in western Transdanubia. It might look authentic to the visitor, but the whole castle is actually a reproduction of the 15th Century original in Vajdahunyad, Transylvania. Late afternoon sun glows on these saints above the entrance, lending a mystical aura to counterbalance to strollers and visitors wandering below.

STEPHEN SPINDER
BUDAPEST
THROUGH MY LENS
A Solitary Perspective

$\mathcal{G}$ellért Monument

1998

Sometimes mistaken for another monumental structure, this image was originally composed in color (see page 136). I was attracted to the contrast of the yellow lamp against the deep iridescent blue sky. It works equally as well in black and white, maintaining its mystery, strength and sense of antiquity.

St. Stephen's Basilica

1997

This monumental neo-Renaissance church is the largest in Budapest. From the ground view, all you can see are the semi-circular chancellery walls and part of the 96 meter tall dome. I was not satisfied with the ground view. I gained access to the rooftop across the street and shot with a 500 mm lens. I was harassed by a curious neighbor until I pointed my lens her way!

STEPHEN SPINDER
BUDAPEST
THROUGH MY LENS
A Solitary Perspective

Fighting the Dragon of Evil

2000

On a cloudless day, I would usually use a red filter while shooting black and white film, to increase the 'white seamless background' effect. Shooting statues such as this one against a cloudless sky renders a clean composition and intensifies the sheer power of such symbols from Hungarian mythical history.

STEPHEN SPINDER

BUDAPEST
THROUGH MY LENS
A Solitary Perspective

Peacock Gates, Gresham Palace

1999

This is an example of the fine ironwork found in Budapest. I cropped this composition so tightly partly because I wanted to really focus on the bird shape... and I couldn't get back any further! My 200 mm lens considerably shortened my depth of field, but you can still see the Chain Bridge in the background.

STEPHEN SPINDER
BUDAPEST
THROUGH MY LENS
A Solitary Perspective

Parliament Dome

2000

The most beautiful, eclectic public buildings in Budapest were erected near Parliament. The famous dome of the parliament guides pedestrians and motorists alike. During an assignment atop a nearby building on Kálmán Imre utca, I grabbed this shot of the cupola. My assignment was to make an interesting composition from atop each Regus building in Central Europe.

STEPHEN SPINDER
BUDAPEST
THROUGH MY LENS
A Solitary Perspective

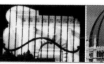

*S*now on Lion's Nose

1999

The architect of these lions prided himself on the realism of the animals. Legend has it that when it was pointed out by a little boy that there were no tongues in the lions' mouths, he became distraught and committed suicide. The only 'tongue' I ever found was the one created by the snow's shape of the lion's nose.

*H*orses, *Heroes' Square*

1998

Armed with my standard lens of the time, a 200 mm Nikor, I would search the city for interesting details. The fierce horses leading the chariots of war are one of four symbolic statues that sit atop the pillars surrounding the square. This image is originally in color, but is equally impressive in black and white.

STEPHEN SPINDER
BUDAPEST
THROUGH MY LENS
A Solitary Perspective

*H*ome, *Andrássy Street*

1998

Andrássy út is the most regal of spokes radiating out from the center of Pest. Most of the grand old homes have been beautifully refurbished, and now house embassies, international law firms, banks, and the infamous former headquarters of the Arrow Cross and secret police, House of Terror.

Flowers, Andrássy Street

1998

Ornate wrought iron gates frame the homes along Andrássy Street with details such as these flowers, underscoring the elegance of the wide boulevard. Framing doorways and balconies, the extraordinary gates on this street exemplifies some of the finest ironwork in Europe.

STEPHEN SPINDER
BUDAPEST
THROUGH MY LENS
A Solitary Perspective

*H*olocaust Memorial, *Wall of Names*

1997

This photograph was actually made in Prague, another fabled city. The number of victims of the Holocaust was enormous there also. Just as thousands of names are recorded on 'leaves' of the memorial in Budapest, here the names of those who perished are hand-painted on a half inch by one inch space.

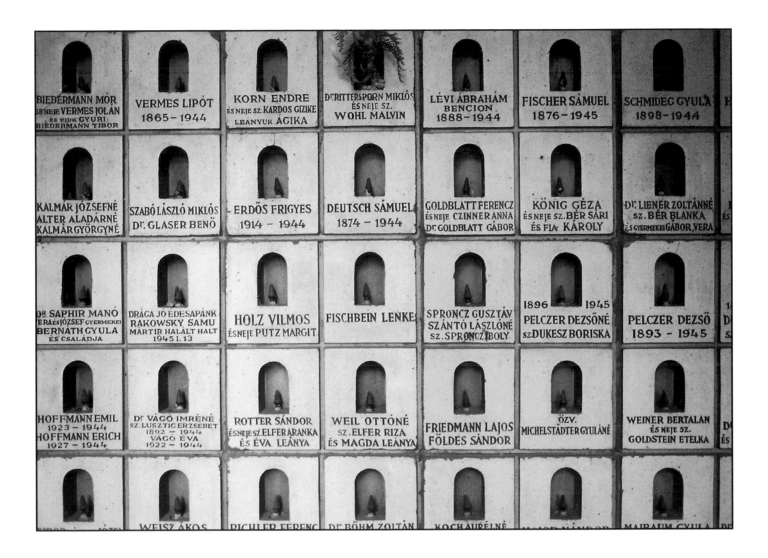

*H*olocaust Rememberance Wall

2000

I was immediately struck by the repetition of pattern formed by these 'boxes'. Over 2000 names are inscribed on this wall behind the Great Synagogue to honor those Jews who died saving others during the Holocaust. A light is contained in each box to signify, in Jewish tradition, hope and faith.

STEPHEN SPINDER
BUDAPEST
THROUGH MY LENS
A Solitary Perspective

Gellért Baths Interior

1997

This is another one of my many unrecognizable views of Budapest, even to the locals. After a bath one morning I made my way upstairs to explore the architecture. I shot from many different angles but when I framed these straight lines against the solid curves, I instinctively knew this would be a striking image.

STEPHEN SPINDER
BUDAPEST
THROUGH MY LENS
A Solitary Perspective

Interior,
Keleti Train Station

1996

Taken in the early morning hours, I was fortunate to get this shot devoid of people, so different from the usual hustle and bustle of trains coming and going from Vienna, Bucharest, and elsewhere. I remember waiting a while for some people to vacate my viewfinder. But if you look closely enough, you may find two...

STEPHEN SPINDER

BUDAPEST
THROUGH MY LENS
A Solitary Perspective

Applied Arts Museum, Vestibule

2001

This is another masterpiece of the great Hungarian Art Nouveau architect Ödön Lechner. He took many of his motifs from ancient Oriental and Indian art since scholars at the time held these to be the origins of the Magyars. Running through the center of the image, the white line you see is actually the edge of a gigantic poster which I incorporated it into the composition.

STEPHEN SPINDER
BUDAPEST
THROUGH MY LENS
A Solitary Perspective

Four Kings under Full Moon

1999

A full moon over Budapest always energizes me. When I looked through my 200 mm lens at three of the Kings at Heroes' Square, I was reminded of the three kings of Bethlehem. I backed up three (meters) to include four

(statues) and moved left to mysteriously place the dome
of the skating rink building in the background.

Large Market Hall

1999

This busy, three-floored market - *Nagy Vásárcsarnok* - was restored to its former working glory in 1994 and once again became a major bonus for Budapest shoppers. The building alone, standing at Fővám Square near the Freedom bridge, is worth a visit.

$\mathcal{K}$eleti, 12:04

1998

This was titled by a client, an attorney with a meticulous sense of time. Of course, I was much more interested in the rhythmic patterns of the repeating arches than I was in the time of day.

STEPHEN SPINDER
BUDAPEST
THROUGH MY LENS
A Solitary Perspective

*M*atthias Church with Crescent Moon

1997

As I walked along Széchenyi rakpart one evening, I noticed a setting crescent moon over the spires of Buda. I quickly headed north in time to 'place' the waxing celestial body anywhere relative to the spire I chose. I didn't realize it then, but I'd inadvertently imposed on this Catholic Church the symbol of the Turkish Empire which once ruled Hungary.

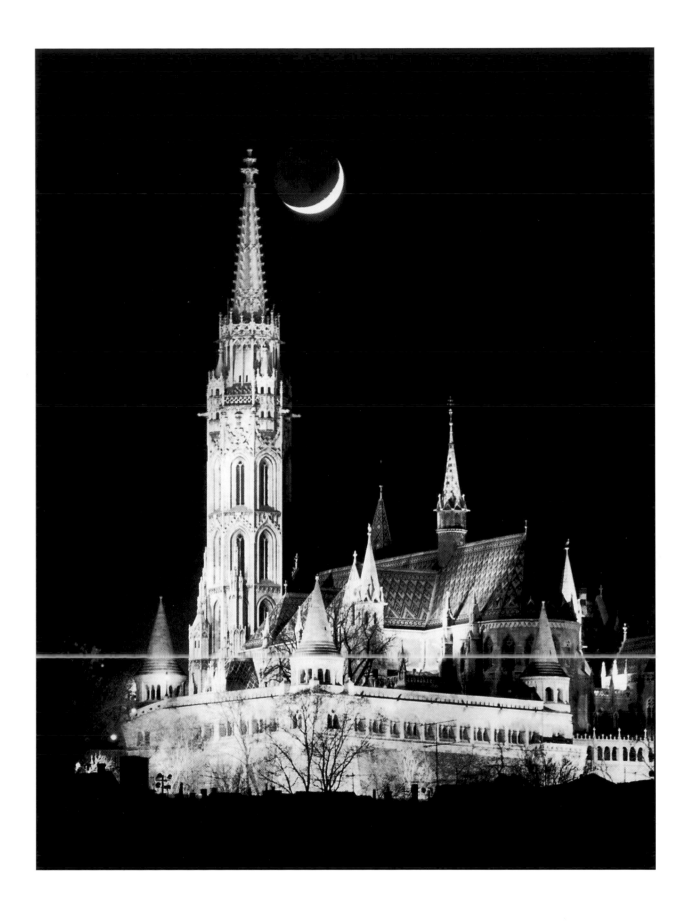

Chain Bridge with Crescent Moon

1995

One of my first serious photographic studies upon moving to Budapest was the Chain Bridge. I never noticed the covered star of the communist era, until a client decided not to purchase the picture for his company because it did not sport the new Hungarian coat of arms. The star on the bridge had been covered since the political changes in 1989, and was replaced with the new coat of arms just a few years later.

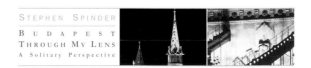

*S*torm Clouds, *Citadel Monument*

1998

During another late afternoon walk along the riverside, black storm clouds hung over the architecture of Buda. I was compelled to sit and watch a while. Dark, ominous... then a clearing. I caught a glimpse of the black silhouette of the Freedom Statue.

When this vision finally appeared, I had about four seconds to record the moment.

STEPHEN SPINDER
BUDAPEST
THROUGH MY LENS
A Solitary Perspective

*M*atthias Church with Fisherman's Bastion

1997

I made this shot at the same time as the image on page 91. This one required a horizontal composition to include Fisherman's Bastion - a treasure of towers and turrets - with the Church of Our Lady.

Árpád Leading the Kings, Heroes' Square

1998

The beloved leader of the Hungarians who led the seven Magyar tribes into the Carpathian basin, seems to be guided by the crescent moon hanging over Heroes' Square.

STEPHEN SPINDER
BUDAPEST
THROUGH MY LENS
A Solitary Perspective

Liberation Monument

2001

This imposing structure, with its palm leaf of victory, is forty meters tall and dominates the Buda skyline. Exploring the complex, I played with a forshortened composition and contrast, and framed the black statue against its white pedestal. This composition, which expresses the monumentality of the structure, was dedicated to the Russians for their courage and might in liberating Budapest at the end of the war.

$\mathcal{L}$ooking under Chain Bridge

1997

After one successful trip to the water's edge a month earlier, I returned to the banks of the Danube on the Pest side. In this shot you can see two of the most popular sights of Buda, Castle Hill and Matthias Church.

Saint Anne's Church, Batthyány Square

1997

Like the storm-clouded sky above the Freedom Statue on page 96, you will find a similar climatic turbulence here. The two shots were taken in the same afternoon. While in the first I'd waited for the storm clouds to clear to get the intense silhouette, in the second I had to wait for the clouds to block the sun again for the dramatic rimmed lighting.

STEPHEN SPINDER
BUDAPEST
THROUGH MY LENS
A Solitary Perspective

*C*ouple along *Széchenyi Rakpart*

1997

At the time of exposure, I didn't realize I had just captured the classic image of love with its timeless element of old age. The Chain Bridge clouded in mist in the background lends itself to this universal theme. I photographed this well dressed, older couple for a few minutes until they

passed me. They told me how they take this afternoon
stroll almost every day.

STEPHEN SPINDER
BUDAPEST
THROUGH MY LENS
A Solitary Perspective

Chain Bridge, Double Vision

1995

Partially double exposed, this proves that an accident can produce a good shot. During the one second exposure, the camera obviously moved. The specular highlights were bright enough to record the movement, appearing doubled, in contrast to the dull light on Matthias Church.

STEPHEN SPINDER

BUDAPEST
THROUGH MY LENS
A Solitary Perspective

*O*belisk, *Heroes' Square*

1997

This magnificent Corinthian column stands in the center of the square. I originally utilized color film and a star filter to emphasize the effects of the setting sun. I feel it has an even more dramatic effect in black and white.

STEPHEN SPINDER

BUDAPEST
THROUGH MY LENS
A Solitary Perspective

Kids Mimicking Statues

1996

Photographing the massive workers' statues in Olympiad Park, I noticed these kids playing nearby. I called them over to try to get them to mimic the shapes of the runners behind them. Even with the help of their curiously amused mother they didn't quite get what the guy with the camera was trying to explain.

*W*oman,
Blaha Lujza Square

1991

She just watched me with suspicion as I moved around low to the ground. The political changes had already occurred, but people were still waiting. She was in the foreground but hundreds of people behind her were also waiting for some major change to take place in the everyday life of Hungarians.

STEPHEN SPINDER
BUDAPEST
THROUGH MY LENS
A Solitary Perspective

Széki Woman, Váci Street

1991

When Hungary's borders were opened in 1989, Transylvanian Hungarians flocked to this pedestrian mall to sell their folklore until the city forced them out around 1994. Erzsi traveled many miles from the Hungarian village of Szék in Transylvania, to reach this lucrative tourist street. Five years after this shot was taken, I went to Szék, and found Erzsi as hospitable and generous as she had been when we first met.

STEPHEN SPINDER

BUDAPEST
THROUGH MY LENS
A Solitary Perspective

Evita Film Set

1996

Everybody wanted in on the movie when Madonna came to town for her leading role in Alan Parker's musical tribute to Eva Peron, but few made it. I was one of them and I'm in three scenes. In one, my face fills half the screen for eight seconds. No cameras were allowed on set, so I concealed my little Nikon zoom 800. This shot was as close as I got to Madonna.

Five Women on Andrássy

2001

These women sit on the city bench in front of the Goethe Institute's coffee house almost every summer day. They relax, gossip, and watch people watch them. Having my coffee, I kept trying to make a shot without drawing the ladies' attention. But in the end, one old posed look completed the picture, as did the old Volkswagen posed in the background.

STEPHEN SPINDER
BUDAPEST
THROUGH MY LENS
A Solitary Perspective

Chester, Tapping for Tourists

1997

In 1997, I helped organize Budapest's first Tap and Lindyhop Dance Festival. We invited Chester Whitmore from California to teach a master class in tap. One day, he attracted crowds of tourists atop Gellért Hill when he asked a Gypsy fiddler to play 'Sweet Georgia Brown' for him.

Dancers

1995

This is the Bartók Folk Ensemble, whose director, Zoli "*Powder*" Nagy, issued the invitation that brought me to Hungary in 1991. He introduced me to many of the dancers on the folk dance scene, and the dances too. That's how I knew approximately when the boots would leave the stage in this one, the *legényes*, or lads' dance.

STEPHEN SPINDER
BUDAPEST
THROUGH MY LENS
A Solitary Perspective

Lenin, Statue Park

1998

The massive Lenin bust dominates the outdoor museum, watching over visitors from every corner. This was a profile that used to make too many appearances around Budapest, but now it is a safely stored relic asleep beyond the city limits.

STEPHEN SPINDER
BUDAPEST
THROUGH MY LENS
A Solitary Perspective

$\mathcal{D}$anubius Fountain, Elizabeth Square

2002

When you emerge from the underground line at Deák Square you are greeted by these peaceful statues sitting under the fountain in the park. This is a usual route for me and I walk by here almost every day, watching them in wonder every time I pass by.

*S*tatue Park *through two*

1998

This small but impressive 'graveyard' park houses many of the great statues that once decorated the city prior to 1989. Unique Soviet-era objects like 'Best of Communism' CDs, 'Game Over' t-shirts, and the last breath of communism sealed in a tin can, can be purchased here.

STEPHEN SPINDER
BUDAPEST
THROUGH MY LENS
A Solitary Perspective

Buda
Royal Palace

2001

In this shot, one can see the National Archives building , the Hungarian National Gallery and, on the right side, the Széchenyi Library, which was founded by Ferenc Széchényi, the father of the famous son István. In this busy late afternoon shot I tried to include in the composition almost as many visual elements as there are volumes (over two million) housed in the building.

Parliament House, Detail

1997

Unlike most of my images of Parliament which show full views of the structure, this extreme close-up of the grandiose pinnacles gives a sense of the impressive detail that covers the building. Like a microcosm of the entire structure, the detail is as mighty as the whole.

STEPHEN SPINDER
BUDAPEST
THROUGH MY LENS
A Solitary Perspective

View from Margaret Bridge

1998

Acclaimed as one of the best photographic viewpoints of the Danube and its imposing banks, this is also a very challenging viewpoint because it presents difficult lighting situations. I chose late afternoon light to accent the grandiose gothic pinnacles of the Parliament. This print was presented to Madeleine Albright, former U.S. Secretary of State, during her visit to Budapest in 2000.

*F*lood at Parliament

2002

The mighty Danube splits Budapest in two and sometimes floods the city. There was a preliminary flood in March of this year, but the most devastating one occured in August, with the water rising to just centimeters below the gates of Parliament.

STEPHEN SPINDER
BUDAPEST
THROUGH MY LENS
A Solitary Perspective

Parliament with Full Moon

1999

I arrived early one evening atop Castle Hill for an obligatory 'full moon over Parliament' shot. With moon's first peak over the horizon, I could see that I had miscalculated my position. It took ten minutes to run to the other end of the Castle District. The celestial body had already risen and faded somewhat from its fiery yellow, but I was fortunate to capture it in this twilight blue.

STEPHEN SPINDER
BUDAPEST
THROUGH MY LENS
A Solitary Perspective

Chain Bridge, Royal Palace

1992

Taken from the typical tourist 'platform' on the Pest side, this was recorded on Kodak transparency film. As usual, I took advantage of that special time of evening just after sunset. If you search long enough, you can find this exact spot. But what you won't find anymore is the old communist star that still decorated the bridge then, though covered by cloth.

STEPHEN SPINDER
BUDAPEST
THROUGH MY LENS
A Solitary Perspective

View from
Mark and Yana's

2001

Visiting some dear friends one summer evening, I walked into their living room, which offers a breathtaking view of the Danube and Buda beyond. Within the hour, the vista was transformed into the most beautiful, picture-perfect postcard shot. With a tripod and calculated exposure, I made the image.

Chain Bridge

1991

From the top of the InterContinental Hotel one notices probably for the first time mountains behind Matthias Church. I was refused permission to go up to the roof, but my journalistic tendencies ensured my eventual success. After two hours and many great shots, I started down but all doors were locked. I pounded on every one until a surprised, irate security guard let me 'in'.

STEPHEN SPINDER
BUDAPEST
THROUGH MY LENS
A Solitary Perspective

Gellért Monument

1998

Sometimes mistaken for another monumental structure, this image was originally composed in color (see page 62-63). I was attracted to the contrast of the yellow lamp against the deep iridescent blue sky. It works equally well in black and white, maintaining its mystery, strength and sense of antiquity.

Freedom Statue, Unparallel Bars

2001

It doesn't seem to matter what time of day or evening, this monument is always crowded with visitors to Budapest. The only way to clear the area of tourists is to administer a little direction, and calculate a long exposure. Originally commissioned by Admiral Horthy for his son, the 14 meter statue was eventually built to Soviet requirements.

STEPHEN SPINDER
BUDAPEST
THROUGH MY LENS
A Solitary Perspective

St. Stephen's Day Fireworks

2001

Photographers claim to plan every shot meticulously, but few will reveal that an afternoon of beer and bad timing can frustrate finding the best view. Because of the thick crowd of revelers, I missed the 'real' view of the fireworks over the Danube. However, I did meticulously calculate

this composition of a statue in silhouette, and the people
perched upon it.

STEPHEN SPINDER
BUDAPEST
THROUGH MY LENS
A Solitary Perspective

Vajdahunyad Castle, Winter

2000

When I made this image of crisp clean morning light, I felt like I was in a winter wonderland. I made it available as a seasonal greeting card, a note card and postcard, as it has become the most sought after photograph in my library, my quintessential Budapest shot.

STEPHEN SPINDER

BUDAPEST
THROUGH MY LENS
A Solitary Perspective

*C*orvina Bird

2000.

Late in the day, I found myself wandering around the Castle District, Buda's old medieval center. I was searching for the late afternoon sun, and it's effects on everything it bathes. The black iron gateway to the Széchenyi library is wrought in the form of a huge butterfly and, sitting warmly on top, the Corvina bird, famous symbol of the famous Renaissance King, Matthias Corvinus.

*R*oyal Palace

1999

The Castle District is the ancient kernel of the capital's right bank settlement, and was the medieval administrative center. I had seen a tapestry of color transform the Buda skyline many times before, and with each sighting promised I would one day capture it.

STEPHEN SPINDER
BUDAPEST
THROUGH MY LENS
A Solitary Perspective

*A*griculural
Museum

2000

The area behind Heroes' Square is a tourist's dream. The only way to photograph there while avoiding people is to look up, or photograph at night. Photographers love that wonderful light phenomenon called twilight - a godsend. Here the saturated yellow hue of the buildings in the Vajdahunyad castle complex provides the perfect color contrast to the iridescent blue sky.

Vajdahunyad Castle

2000

'Photography' means the study of light. On a summer evening in Budapest, around 9pm, twilight bathes the sky in iridescent blue light. Because this quality of light only lasts a few minutes, I studied it, and had time to make about six frames, including this one.

STEPHEN SPINDER
BUDAPEST
THROUGH MY LENS
A Solitary Perspective

*Prince Eugene
of Savoy*

1995

When color film is exposed longer than recommended, an effect called 'reciprocity' occurs, whereby colors as they appear are surrealistically changed on film. It is not uncommon to get green skies and magenta statues.

STEPHEN SPINDER

BUDAPEST
THROUGH MY LENS
A Solitary Perspective

*S*ynagogue,
Rumbach Sebestyén Street

1997

*A*pplied Arts Museum,
Interior

2001

1848, March 15th Anniversary

1998

It was on these stairs that Sándor Petőfi gave his famous speech which incited Hungarians to rise up against the Habsburg rule. Because of the massive crowds, I was unable to get any closer to these celebrations at the National Museum, but did manage to get higher. Precipitously perched on top of a guard gate, I was able to include everyone on the wide colonnaded vestibule. Everything was perfect, even those Hungarian flags, partially blocking my view.

*1*0th Anniversary of *American Chamber of Commerce in Hungary*

1999

Armed with a panorama camera (constant exposure during the 270° rotation of the lens) and with access to the upper floors of Parliament, I was allowed this unique perspective and an opportunity to include in one shot many of the international business leaders in Budapest in one frame. Technical assistance by Ferenc Nika, Studioline Kft.

Blue Fog

2000

I awoke early one morning to find my street had disappeared into fog. I grabbed my camera and headed 'somewhere'. Chain Bridge, I thought. When I arrived, the bridge was almost completely obliterated by this eerie blue fog. In my mind's eye was the memory of a similar shot I had made one year earlier. So as not to waste the moment, I burned off two rolls in about twenty minutes. It was one of the last shots I made that day, through my lens...